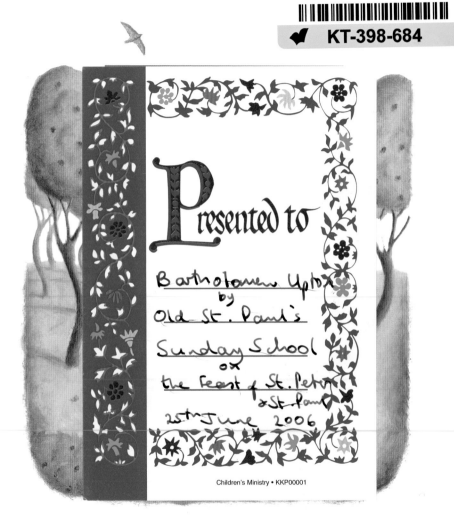

Presented to

Bartholomew Upton
by
Old St. Paul's
Sunday School
on
the Feast of St. Peter
& St. Paul
25th June 2006

Children's Ministry • KKP00001

For every cup and plateful,
Lord, make us truly grateful

Written and compiled by Lois Rock
All unattributed prayers by Lois Rock
are copyright © Lion Hudson
Illustrations copyright © 1999 Alison Jay
This edition copyright © 2005 Lion Hudson

The moral rights of the author and illustrator
have been asserted

A Lion Children's Book
an imprint of
Lion Hudson plc
Mayfield House, 256 Banbury Road,
Oxford OX2 7DH, England
www.lionhudson.com
ISBN 0 7459 4917 7

First edition 2005
10 9 8 7 6 5 4 3 2 1 0

A catalogue record for this book is available
from the British Library

Typeset in 15/19 Venetian 301 BT
Printed and bound in China

The illustrations in this book were selected
from *The Lion Treasury of Children's Prayers*,
published by Lion in 1999.

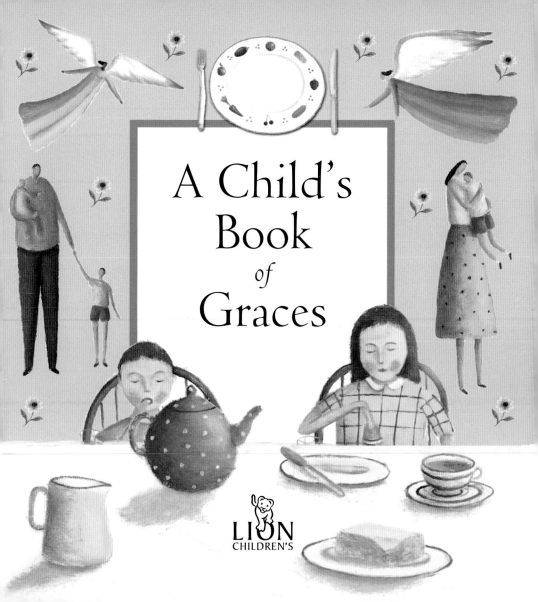

A Child's
Book
of
Graces

LION
CHILDREN'S

In the morning

Morning is here,
The board is spread,
Thanks be to God,
Who gives us bread.

Anonymous

For health and strength
and daily food,
we praise your name,
O Lord.

Traditional

Alone and quietly

Dear God,
I gratefully bow my head
To thank you for my daily bread,
And may there be a goodly share
On every table everywhere. Amen

A Mennonite children's prayer

Thank you, dear God,
for the blessing of quietness.
Thank you, dear God,
for the blessing of food.
Thank you, dear God,
for the blessing of your
encircling love.

Our family

Thank you, dear God,
that we can meet together
and eat together
and pray together
and stay together.

We are hungry,
We have food,
We are family,
God is good.

Friends around the table

For our food and those who prepare it;
For health and friends to share it,
We thank you, Lord.

Anonymous

Let us take a moment
To thank God for our food,
For friends around the table
And everything that's good.

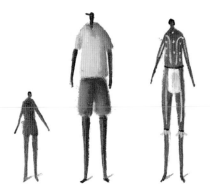

Out of doors

We thank thee, Lord, for happy hearts,
For rain and sunny weather,
We thank thee, Lord, for this our food,
And that we are together.

Emilie Fendall Johnson

Us and this: God bless.

A Quaker grace

Our Daily Bread

Heavenly Father,
Give us this day our daily bread.

From Luke 11:2–3

We remember the day that Jesus accepted a gift
of five loaves and two fish. He looked up to heaven
and thanked God for them. Then he broke them
and gave them to his disciples to share with the
crowd of people. They all ate and had enough.

From Luke 9:16–17

Hunger satisfied

We give thanks for our hunger,
We give thanks for our food,
We give thanks for enough of each
To do our bodies good.

For food in a world where many walk in hunger;
For faith in a world where many walk in fear;
For friends in a world where many walk alone,
We give you humble thanks, O Lord.

A Girl Guide world hunger grace

Harvest thanksgiving

Bless the earth
and bless the seed:
We have all the food we need.

Bless the sunshine,
bless the air:
We have food enough to share.

Harvest time is gold and red:
Thank God for our daily bread.

All good gifts around us
Are sent from heaven above,
Then thank the Lord, O thank the Lord,
For all his love.

Matthias Claudius (1740–1815),
translated by Jane Montgomery Campbell (1817–78)

Thank you everyone

God bless those who grew all this food.
    May they enjoy good food too.
God bless those who helped harvest this food.
    May they enjoy good food too.
God bless those who transported this food.
    May they enjoy good food too.

God bless those who sold us this food.
   May they enjoy good food too.
God bless those who prepared this food.
   May they enjoy good food too.
God bless us as we eat this food.
   May we enjoy this good food and be thankful.

From around the world

Each time we eat,
may we remember God's love.

A Chinese grace

The bread is warm and fresh,
The water cool and clear.
Lord of all life, be with us,
Lord of all life, be near.

An African grace

Thank you for the rice that sustains my body:
most honourable food.

Thank you for the love that sustains my soul:
most honourable God.

A Japanese grace

From long ago

To God who gives our daily bread
A thankful song we raise,
And pray that he who sends us food
May fill our hearts with praise.

Thomas Tallis (c. 1505–85)

Bless me, O Lord, and let my food
strengthen me to serve thee, for
Jesus Christ's sake.

Isaac Watts (1674–1748)

Be present at our table, Lord,
Be here and everywhere adored;
Thy creatures bless and grant that we
May feast in paradise with thee.

John Cennick (1718–55)

After eating

Thank you, dear God, for the food I have eaten
and enjoyed. Thank you for the comfortable
feeling of being satisfied. I am grateful for
this and all your blessings.

Thank you for good food
that makes me strong:
strong to do good.